To Gill & Rowland,
with thanks
for your support
and kindness.
Pamela Bakker

A Web of Cries

by

Pamela Bakker

Chapbook series published by:

Pipers' Ash Limited

www.supamasu.com

CHIPPENHAM ◆ WILTSHIRE ◆ ENGLAND

SN15 4BW

'Salisbury Edition'
ISBN 1-902628-55-1

Contents:

I Forget-me-Nots

II Politics to Porridge

III Talking in Tongues

I   Forget-me-Nots

Bedroom Eyes

I used to be told I had bedroom eyes,
Inviting, alluring, my brilliant surprise
Causing several an admirer instantly to rise
Whenever I'd happen to enter a room.

Now all I see are the cracks
In the ceiling, paint
That is peeling, and the
Hideous pink roses of this rented room.

A haunt of gloom this soulless tomb;
A pink and blue stripe strangles
Three walls, while the fourth
Is splattered pink shite.

My bedroom eyes are growing dimmer;
My limbs shrink slimmer as
Hair loses shimmer and
Brain feels thinner.

You have stolen my sight,
Vandalized my right to a
Peaceful plight in this
Our eternal fight for life.

Garish pink roses in ugly poses
Blur into a visual epitaph:
My once beautiful bedroom eyes
Have unwillingly metamorphoseyesed into
Bed, room, lies.

In the Midst of Life
For my Mother

Midway the journey of this life I was 'ware
That I had strayed into a dark forest,
And the right path appeared not anywhere.
Ah, tongue cannot describe how it oppressed,
This wood, so harsh, dismal and wild, that fear
At thought of it strikes now into my breast.
So bitter it is, death is scarce bitterer.
Dante, Inferno, Canto I

All around me, Tygers burning bright,
Leopards crouching in the clear moonlight;
Creeping, shrieking, drooping, swooping –
Life at night giving way to fright,
Terror, panic, quivering, shivering.

A human being
In the midst of Life
Is not well prepared
For so engulfing a lair.

But there I stood
Afraid and confused,
Disdained, abandoned,
Cruelly abused.

My body had left me
But was still there;
My brain, rearranged,
Still dwelt amidst hair.

And yet this lair
Gripped me tight,
Tight in the deepest
Forest of the night.

At last I could see
I was dis-eased,
But without a map,
Without a clue -

For as I soon learnt
I could not DO.

Finally I sat and then lay down,
Realizing I had to accept
This foreign ground.
There I lay and lay and lay
Until one beautiful dawning day,
By the light of the rising sun,
My eyes opened and at once I knew
The disease at long last was undone.
And I gave thanks
To the heat of this star,
To the steady faith
Of friends near and far;
I cried with joy
That I was still alive,
And rose from the ground
Ready to thrive.

By the radiance of the sun
I strode along the path
Out of the woods to my new home,
And there climbed up happily
To the Future,
My throne.

Nuts

Am I so very strange
For this tingling in my feet?
Do you believe me deranged
For non-stop pain in my brain?
Does my unidentified viral infection
Make me suitable for a section?
And is it so weird to have this
High-pitched siren in my ear?
Do my muscles twitch and ache,
Or is that just a spectacular fake?
And is the fact
I can no longer walk,
Though sit and speak,
A fantastical feat?

All these things you have implied today,
Undermining my dignity,
Shredding my integrity.
So, Doctor, tell me then,
Since you, so obviously qualified,
And wish your patient mollified,
Would your psychiatric referral
Perhaps not be better
For one of those creatures
Who twitters away with nuts in its mouth,
What is it…oh yes, a squirrel?

The Ravelled Sleeve of Care

Another friend bows out of my life
For no apparent reason,
When once we used to laugh and dine
Sharing too many bottles of wine;
Trips to the theatre we'd take together,
Exchanging friendship and ideas,
Foolishly I hoped that these
Would carry on forever.

No apparent reason, I said,
Though that is not quite true;
It should have read:
One enormous reason
Which I am powerless to undo.

Just as each night knits up
The ravelled sleeve of care,
So my nights offer me
Slumber not as fair
With an illness that feeds
Upon the caress of a night,
An illness that refuses
To put my body to right.

Each morn my bag of bones
Will scarcely move, while
My nerves, all awry,
Vie with twitching muscles.

Each morn the continual intrigue
To discover the root of
Incessant fatigue,
As well as bodily malfunction,
Not to mention the continual effort
To discover the reason I've missed
The hundred and fiftieth luncheon.

M.E. hath murdered sleep,
And everyday I must now wear
This shrunken, sleeveless garment,
This habit of pain and despair.
M.E. hath murdered sleep
And with it most of my friends
Who, so entrenched in their own affairs,
Have long ceased pretending to care.
A handful I now have left,
A well worn pack I'd never throw down,
Not for riches, the earth, an instant cure,
Nor even a bejewelled crown.

M.E. hath murdered my life
For four years now –
And yet somehow
I know one day that
All the perfumes of Arabia,
Some potent potion of thought and medicine,
Shall wash away this dreadful disease,
Knitting once again my missing sleeves.
And I shall realise surely then
The greater loss
Must be, in the end,
Not to have lost,
But to have failed to remain
A true friend.

The Butterfly Bush

Resplendent in its purple glory,
Siren to orange, black, yellow and red
Wingèd creatures who suck and are fed
The most delicious of nectars,
Sweeter for even the lotus-eaters.
These flutterbys fanning most luscious colour,
Remind me too that I one day,
Like the caterpillar,
Shall emerge triumphal from my own story.

Billy's Back

Beauteous wingèd creature,
I've just spied you on the gutter again
My friend, my good omen,
My orange-beaked beacon,
Showing spring is under your wing,
Blowing your black radiance and
Whistling to me that seasons do change,
That hope springs eternal within
Our oft coal-coloured hearts.
Winter is over, though suffering still smoulders,
But soon shall be snuffed out:
For Billy's back, with his orange spout.
He heralds rejuvenation, even salvation,
Giving my every day companionship
And transforming illness, with his song,
Into a memory long forgotten, long gone.

There is No Magic in this Mountain

There is no magic in this mountain,
This peak of despair and pain,
This mountain where one, like Sisyphus,
Starts each day with no apparent gain –
Only the same boulder to push up and up…
But of course 'pushing' is something
Up with which we cannot put!

There is no magic in this mountain,
No thermometers to 'look forward to',
Just the same readings everyday -
In every way the opposite to Hans' child's play:
No balconies to take in the fresh mountain air,
Or to recline on in the afternoons after chocolate éclair.
We're lucky in the winter for ten minutes outside,
      if indeed we dare.

There is no magic in this mountain,
Though our bodies do not die,
Our lives are blasted nonetheless, point blank, in the eye.
For we are incapable of attending evening soirées,
Lectures, meetings, cards, toboggan escapades;
We cannot dine 'ensembles', joining in discourse;
Some days all we can do is be spoon-fed a single course.

There is no magic in this mountain,
This Everest we face: no diagnosis, no prognosis,
(Though, tragically, some overdoses.)
There may well be wars on the ground,
But most, even those willing, could never make it down.
All that we may do before this mammoth, slouching beast
Is delve deep inside our aching souls to where our dreams may feast.

Forget Me Not

Forget me not,
She wrote in the sand,
For my body is sailing
To a far-off land.
What I'll find there
I haven't a clue -
But my task must be
To search for my spirit,
And return to these shores
My body bound with it.
A map I lack,
So I may lose my track.
If I do, then remember one thing:
I have loved this life
Despite everything.

Part of M.E.

One day I decide:
I'll shake hands with
Loneliness, become its friend;
It seems better that way
Rather than fighting to no end.

The next day I'm back
To punching, kicking, screaming
In its ugly, mocking face:
'I'd rather die a thousand deaths
Than be trapped in your embrace.'

The following day it's the turn of tears,
Drenching my new feather pillow,
While my heart aches its usual ache –
The one these days I cannot shake –
For someone, anyone, myself... gone.

Whether friendship, anger or sorrow,
Loneliness has become my every tomorrow,
Some days gently holding my hand,
Others, like a ghost, unable to scan.
So I listen to music, stare outside, whatever I can
In the never-ending hope
That loneliness will metamorphose:
Add an 'A', lose the 'li'
And find love for my aloneness
As an integral part of me.

3000 Miles

I've not been 'waving' for a long time now,
But somehow the distance has enabled you
To see only the brave and cheery show.
How, after all this time, can you not see
I've long since let that go?

From 3000 miles much may be hidden,
The Atlantic concealing my days,
Especially from family who desperately wish
To be blinded by ocean spray.

For a week or two, sometimes a month,
They'd appear: propping pillows,
Arranging flowers, popping pills
To dim their view of my horrific ills –
The twitching, the shaking,
The blindness, the aching,
The panics, the fevers,
The neurological dysfunction.

Unctuous would be these visits,
Swathed in virtue - and, 'Oh so exhausting',
But to me each felt like minutes.
And then they'd leave,
With meticulous speed,
Their hands waving,
So solicitous in braving
The 3000 miles ahead.

Yet their heads were always way above water,
While mine sunk deeply in the bed.

Pain

Chronic
Supersonic
Defying all tonic,
This insane pain,
This runaway train in my brain.

Aching shooting stabbing,
Grabbing any new pill thrown before me.

Searing jeering leering
Smearing my mouth
With phrases obscene –
This profane pain
This profane, inane bloody pain
Which disdains even a name.

Keenly grinding blinding throbbing
Sobbing oft relieves the interminable jabbing.

Surely some cursèd spite
Must drive this torturous pain,
My mark of Cain.
For over two years,
Day in, day out,
I have endured
A wrenching clenching
Tightening frightening
Crunching punching
Flinching wincing
Hammering clamouring
St-st-stammering
Pain.

Despite all this, O Divine Light,
I've not lost faith in your might,
And therefore shall endure
This weighty smite
Until I am delivered into
Heavenly respite.

Panegyric

Katie:
My carer, healer, friend,
My warrior, defender to the end;
The soother of my pain,
With never expectation
Or hope of any gain.

Katie – who never leaves me,
Is with me day and night,
Has proven more than a carer,
More than a friend,
A species never rarer,
My staff that never bends.

Katie wades with me
'Through thick and thin', they say;
For us mostly molasses,
Yet ever she remains
The foil of any Cassius,
Her loyalty miraculous.

Katie, in one sweeping stroke,
Feeds me, cleans me, soothes my brow,
Brightens my life with innate know-how;
Her task so steep
Even Sisyphus would
Balk at such a feat.

Katie cares lovingly,
Gently,
Compassionately,
Selflessly,
Silently –
A true Cordelia is my friend.

Flow My Tears

O, Let me weep for this reeled off scene:

Flow my tears for all the films I have not seen,
For the stages strutted upon I have not been;
Flow my tears for three years of history that have passed me by
Without so much as a wave or a cry.
O, Let me weep for the world turning, evolution churning,
For New York burning;
For all the events that have made dents in this life,
From which I have been cut off by a carving knife.

Flow my tears for the blind mouse I have been,
For all the friends I have not seen,
O, Let me weep for those I have lost,
That huge gaping hole, that most dreadful toll.
Let me weep too for all the lovers never met,
For all the rendez-vous never kept.

Flow my tears for I have been in bed, bed, bed,
Dead on the outside, re-wired in my head;
Flow my tears for the medical profession,
For its ignorance, disdain and lack of progression
About a disease affecting 150,000,
And that's just counting this tiny island.

Flow my tears for the books I've not written, let alone read,
For all the ideas now entombed under this bed.
O, Let me weep into this damnèd bed
In which my prime years are now dead, dead, dead.

Mostly though, if you must flow, then start flowing
For the life I want living,
The songs I want singing,
The birth I want giving.
Flow these salty, watery drops
And cleanse my heart, my mind, my spirit,
Purge my body from this enforced hibernation,
And bring me through Life's gates with celebration.

New Year's Eve

I've always hated you
You frightful night,
But especially now, lying in bed
With time's wingèd chariot
Flying through my head.

For three years now I've been in this state,
Barely able to walk, to think, to relate;
If I were as astute as Thomas Mann,
I'd write of Time with words so clever,
I'd philosophise myself out of this ruined endeavour
Called Life – my life –
My broken line of Time.

But for now I shall think of
A solution, some mundane way
To evaporate this ludicrous
Heavy day. I shall think:
Tomorrow I'll wake in
The exact same way,
And pick up where I left off,
With the same hope, the same dismay.

And perhaps I'll realize that
New Year's Eve is a fraud:
An excuse for believing that
Time belongs to us – a gift from God,
And in that way is somehow real,
When we all should know
Our every second's a steal.

Driving Not Too Far

I remember when you
Came in September and
You pushed me in my chair,
Making fun, as usual, of my messy, curly hair;
And we rode in the car –
Not too, too far – but
Enough to celebrate
This disease was not my fate.

And I remember you
Placed your hand upon my shoulder,
Despite I being older,
You could now assume
The role of 'big sister',
And in fun take sweet revenge
For years of tussles and 'sunburn twisters'.

Just that squeeze on my shoulder
Is enough to make me weep,
Remembering your nurture
During nights I couldn't sleep,
Not to mention your wicked cakes
I wasn't supposed to eat!
But now you won't see me –
My disease has scared you so
That, like a distorting mirror,
I'm a place you dare not go.

So I lie here and I miss you,
I kiss your golden hair,
And curl beside you while
You sleep, whispering in your ear
That despite my deserted shoulder,
I still am the older and perhaps
Could show you the monster's
Not as scary as you fear.
But most of all I'm wishing
We were riding in that car,
Our silence full of love,
Just enjoying being together,
The cows, the wind, the heather.

Frain Bog

She poises her pen,
Her white coat shimmering;
I sit there coolly,
Though impatience is simmering.

'How are you today?
Any new symptoms?'

'Never better, thank you,
despite this year-long infection.'

'Good, then I'll just check –
is the light giving off a glare?'

'Yes – could you turn it off?
It's hurting my hair.'

'Do you suffer from brain fog?'

'Excuse me?'

'Do you ever suffer from brain fog?'

'Am I afraid of toilets?
Of course not.
M.E. is a NOT a scatologic...
psych – psychological disorder.'

'No, no, I mean, do you ever suffer
from confusion, brain fatigue?'

'Ever... n-never before.'

'O.K. Moving along...
How much can you now read in one sitting?
Can you still do crosswords, a bit of knitting?'

'I've already told you:
I DON'T suffer from bain frog.
My muscles ache – Can we address that?'

'But of course –
First I'd just like for a minute to backtrack…'

'Look, my mile is going a mind a minute –
could we please move forward?
For one thing, my sore is really throat today
and it hurts to talk.'

'So, conversing is confusing,
I see perhaps your brain does balk…'

'Sorry, I'm too t-tired to walk – talk –
talk any more – as you can see,
I'm not at my best –
right now I really must rest.'

I Lie Here Dying

I lie here dying in a crypt,
Each day like a fatal nail hitting
This tomb, this bed, this room,
To steel me to earth's mortal floor.

Our days are numbered we all know,
Yet in this paralysed state
Each second, minute, hour, date,
Amplify my personal hell,
Like an unnatural tolling knell.

M.E., like death, steals our fleeting time
Faster it seems than we know to be real,
Yet feeling slower than some blackened hearse
Bearing away my wilting verse.

Remembering Me

Nostalgia creeps in
Through the back door,
Stealthily as a ghost
Seeping up through the floor.

Unbidden, it whispers,
It caresses my ears,
Reminding me of the past -
Those faraway years.

With a pin it pricks memory
Unearthing a store
Of long pent up feelings,
Of events of yore.

Events I'd forgotten,
Trivial things, like
Coffee on the beach,
Listening to Grecian crickets sing.

Like the filthy alleyway
Leading to one of my homes,
Like the feel of swimming,
Or making angels in snow.

A piazza in Bologna
Where I sat an entire day,
Drinking in Italy
And the scenes of that play.

Hiking the Rockies,
And whistling away bears;
Reaching the summit,
Feeling free as the air.

How I wish I could
Make them all vanish,
These reminders of a life
That for now is banished.

But perhaps in twenty years
I shall think back to this life -
This one full of anguish and strife -
And feel nostalgia,
Not for the pain,
But for the gift of time
I had to remember again.

A Void

A void am I to you I now see,
Though my body visible, the insides empty.

At Easter time when I was little,
We'd paint pretty eggs, and blow out the middle.

Now I sit, a lump on a bed,
With a body disabled, but an explosive head.

Yet all you will see are the pictures I paint,
The stories I write, the verse I create.

The true voice speaking from my soul
Makes you pack your bags for so heavy a toll.

Pretty Pam, isn't she lovely and sweet,
She'll surely return – 'til then 'Bonne nuit'.

So I continue to sit, a virtual void,
To those I love most: a stranger to avoid.

Fair

That life is unfair
Is a lesson best learnt
Before the age of eighteen.

Yet somewhere persists
A whisper, a kiss,
That life will be fair for me.

At twenty-five, believing our lives
Continue to thrive, a shadow casts
Its first cold blast of uncertainty.

By thirty we're sailing,
Though perhaps not waving,
And wondering what the hell is going wrong.

At thirty-five a pivotal point:
Too many paths possible to take -
Finalities glaring, crucially at stake.

At the prime of my time
I was unexpectedly slain
By a fierce disease riddled with pain.

Incurable, (though some symptoms
Treatable) this dragon, this gorgon,
This most outrageous fortune.

At first I wallowed in a pool of tears,
Lamenting my lost most fertile years;
I cried, I sighed, shouted, screamed.

I cursed my fate, I began to hate
My ruined life, the slings and arrows,
Pitying my most plentiful woes.

Then one mid-March morning in bed,
I turned my head towards the window
And beheld the most beauteous sight.

A wee fair robin pecking the pane
Suddenly melted my broken heart,
And I cried and cried, unburdening my smart.

A turning point occurred that day,
(Some may call it an epiphany)
But from that point forward
No longer did I curse my plight,
Cry with fright, despise my lot.
I realised finally, after some thought,
That arrows are merely arbitrary flings,
That fairness has nothing to do with life,
But robins will always most fairly sing.

To Peel A Potato

What serendipity to hang the washing
On a sunny, spring fresh morning;
What extravagance to gather apples,
To wash them and do the coring;
What pleasure to slice and cook tomatoes;
What happiness to peel a potato.

Such common tasks that seem so menial and boring
Are yet beyond my wildest dreams,
But shall in future be performed
With thanks and
Adoring.

Thirty Seconds

Every morning as I gently wake,
My mind straddling the gates of
Semi-reality: comfort and pain,
I am given thirty seconds where
Life seems full of hope, happiness,
And, most of all, is blissfully plain.

These seconds are a gift from above,
An answered prayer, an effusion of love,
Wherein I feel eager to start the day,
To do my work, to rest, to play;
It is a piece of heaven in my head
Wafting lazily throughout the bed.

Suddenly, as if from a fright,
My eyes bolt open and hit the light –
The so-oft cited 'light of day'
When the thirty seconds vanish
Into never-land, and my happiness,
Like butter, melts into dismay.

Dismay for this day I must now face,
This day choked by illness, devoid of grace.
This day in which again I must
Muster courage, tenacity and patience;
But, most importantly, hope: hope for those
Thirty seconds that shall visit me again,
The following morning, my eyes still closed.

Femme Sur Un Oreiller

I am
Woman on a Pillow;
Not mother,
Not lover,
Nor colleague,
Nor friend;
Simply splodge on a bed
With angular head –
Angles of myself
Discerned only by
Contorted view:
Twisting the mirror
I find eyes askew,
Two lips parted,
Body unrecognisable
But for sizeable features -
Like alien creatures -
Drawn into odd poses,
Into differing frames,
And hence the loss
Even of my name;
I am just
Being
woman on a pillow.

Outside At Last

Outside,
At last,
Though my body inert
Disabled in a chair,
The wind weaves melodies
Randomly through my hair.

Odours, pungent
Explode in my nose,
And despite the autumn
I gaze at rose after rose.

Fields of hay,
Fields of cows,
Embrace my vision,
Dazzle my view,
And the world suddenly
Is born again new.

Chestnuts, acorns,
Lavender, rosemary -
I clutch and smell and
Feel joy to carry
Such precious gifts
I have so long missed,
Three years dissolve
And the future I kiss.

Swiftly Pass Me By

Finally I have surged forward –
Pushed the boulder to the top;
Four years it only took to heave this
Piece of leaden igneous rock.
But here I stand, boulder in hand,
Admiring the view, feeling free as a bird,
Whistling 'phew!' Whistling a few
Songs of joy for this momentous day,
For having resisted all temptation
To seek shelter during Noah's flood,
Falling to the ground, a mound of earth
   and blood.

Now I've admired the view, my body spent,
My mind is up for rent: do I let go the boulder
And climb back down – consolidate my feat
Once again upon firm ground?
Do I allow my body and mind to rest,
As I know I should: rest, pace, rest, pace…
That ghastly chant inscribed inside;
Or do I follow that swift, enchant him here,
Let fall my body on wings so clear –
Clear, free and light as day, swiftly with him
Fly away – borne for once, unshackled by fear?

II *Politics to Porridge*

One

One car bomb and one tiny child is killed.

Six policemen shot dead across a divided field;
Sixteen-year old mangled by explosives in his hand;
600 bodies in unmarked grave found in no-man's land;
6000 from near and afar, victims on the 11th day;
6,000,000 rounded up and tortured in the most heinous way.

How many more zeros
Before humanity learns
There is no point in pretending
That men can be heroes?
How many bombs
Must be dropped?
How many terrorists
Never stopped?
How many wars will
Have to be won
Before we realize
That numbers have
Always counted,
Always start at
One

One tiny ticking unborn heart…

Golden Glowing

It is Easter again, my beautiful one,
A time when the great floppy bunny
Should have been hiding eggs for fun.
A time when you and I would have
Painted blown-out eggs together and
Hung them around our home on pegs.
A time to have celebrated the miracle of your birth,
To have laughed and danced, hugged and kissed,
Enjoying the pleasures of Easter with mirth,
Thanking the Lord for all our blessings and bliss.

Instead I lie here, myself a blown-out egg,
Like on that most terrible day when
They wrenched you from between my legs.
There are no pegs in my house now,
No eggs - just grief shaping my brow.
No joy, screeches, whelps of laughter,
Only tears, and the sharpest dagger in my heart -
A dagger that likes to dance and twist -
Reminding me in the cruellest way,
That you, my love, in flesh no longer exist.

But, like Jesus who ascended,
I'm sure in heaven He has befriended
The cherub that I lost, enveloping
You in His arms: His love, my love showing
Our own trinity golden glowing.

Nobility Unstirred

Telling you I love you,
Eyes pretending not to hear,
Except a slight betrayal:
The minute twitch of an ear.

Eyes almost closed now,
Yet I persist in blowing my heart
Across most beautiful softest fur.
I'll go along then, my Egyptian goddess,
And ignore the faint murmur of your purr.

Sylvie

One rainy April day,
Which could have swung either way,
Sylvie came to sit on my lap,
And started to purr and purr away.

I placed my hand upon her head
And held it there the whole afternoon,
Fearing if I took it away,
The day could go the other way.

The other way, during the cruelest month,
Is not one I like to dwell on much;
So on that rainy afternoon,
I thanked Jesus for feline touch.

Alas

A church in Hythe I visited once
Where pilgrims to Canterbury lost their way.
On a hilltop stood an odd little vault
Where hundreds of skulls stared the tourists out;
Live eyes peeping while skin all creeping
At these dead reminders of our mortal being.
I, myself, felt lucky to be alive,
Staring at skulls that day in Hythe;
But I could not help wondering
How mine would look when
One day my mortal frame I shook.
'Alas, poor Pamela,' would anyone say?
Or would I be forgotten, dissolved into clay?
Did anyone really know me well?
Or would drinks be fast flowing
At the tolling of my knell?
It's hard to say, but on that day
I felt an affinity with the individuality
Of each strangely beautiful head,
And hoped they were peaceful
In their odd vaulted bed.

My Lover Told Me

My lover told me one fine day
We'd sail to a land far away,
Where ancient ghosts haunted castles
And people wore hats with golden tassels.

My lover told me one fine day
That he'd pick me up and whisk me away,
To Paris in the spring at its best,
Though we'd only make love and ignore the rest.

My lover whispered one fine night
We'd visit the Alhambra bathed in moonlight,
And slip along its gilded floors
Peering through exquisite doors.

My lover told me all these things
While foolish I believed in rings,
Which of course never appeared,
And just as surely, he turned queer.

History Condemned

'Au clair de la lune, mon ami Pierrot;
Prêtez – moi le penn pour écrire un mot:
About your tragic loss of not securing the vote –
The vote you bought by selling Nazi trinket things –
Poor poor Le Penn, your nasty rattle stings.

In Holland they are marching to mourn one right and fair;
Please move away so we may clear the square.
The square so right and measured,
The square obscene au clair;
With colourful banners, propaganda flared.

Au clair de la lune le monde devient encore fou:
Full of history repeating, vomiting its past.
A past condemned to madness and far-right neo-Nazz;
Mon ami Pierrot I fear, we've not seen the last;
Prêtez – moi ta plume for another blast.'

Did I Ever Tell You?

Did I ever tell you
During those long seven years,
That my heart wept and bled
Night after night in the same bed?

Did I ever tell you
How everyday I'd try to love you,
To mend our 'happy' home,
When all you wanted was football and to be alone?

Did I ever tell you
That you were never very clever;
How you always looked upon our problems
Only as my own?

Did I ever tell you
How you broke not just my heart,
But my spirit too,
When I found her letter in the pocket of your sweater?

Did I ever tell you
That you were my sentence,
My self-inflicted wound,
The purgatory my subconscious put me through?

Did I ever tell you
That you partly are the reason I've been trapped
Three years disabled in this bed,
Confusion constantly riddling my head?

Did I ever tell you,
Perhaps most importantly,
That as well as my nemesis
You have now become my genesis?

And did I ever tell you
That despite ailing with M.E.,
I feel for the first time ever
That I am getting better?

And the joyous freedom that has come
For having finally left you.

Oh, and

Did I ever tell you
I too never said those
Vows with a smile upon my face?
Or enjoyed a single moment as I
Rejoiced with an opponent;
Celebrating what I now see as an
Egregious mistake.

The Lie in the Pie

Like Pinocchio's nose,
His grows and grows,
Right up to the sky
This lie in the pie.
Where will it stop?
Nobody knows – nobody's nose
Grows as tall and proud;
(Shame it can't be smothered by a shroud)
Such a great story
That Land of Soaps and Glory.

Are we to believe
(And not be deceived)
He was elected fairly?
Fairly and squarely?
Ask a few people
Living down south –
They'll tell you how
Pinocchio's nose stifled
The mouth of the south;
And others too will tell you
How it grew so tall,
It finally slew them all.

Pregnant Pause

Pregnant,
Pause,
'I'm so sorry', she says with pity,
An anguished cry fills the room
'Are you saying all is over?'
My pride, my joy,
My four-leafed clover?
Pause -
'I'm afraid it is.'
An insensible doom
Soon mummifies
My tightening womb.

I am dead:
A wandering ghost,
Empty, discarded,
A forgotten tomb.
My soul, turned to leather,
Merely scuffs the pavement in greying weather.
Now these streets seem so mean, so forlorn,
Where once I squirreled in happiest anticipation,
The stuff and food of every girl's imagination.

Kilburn High Street is bleak in November,
Cold and bitter,
With scowling faces shuffling litter.
An old lady falls – I rush to help her,
But my outstretched hand offers unwanted shelter.
Somehow this comes as no surprise:
How could I offer nurture
When the tiniest of hearts,
The most precious of lives,
Decided I was unfit to proffer a future?

I must to home to bury my body,
Neglected, empty, a looted tomb.
Even my soul has left me now,
Flown this neglected desolate room
Where once a throne
Awaited a prince -
A cradle still lies,
Unmoved ever since.

In bondage to my pain,
Like Prometheus
Who tried to steal the flame,
But chained by my own guilt and self-blame.
Not woman enough to create a perfect child,
I now hang my head in shame,
My desperation growing wild.

In bondage to my pain
Never-ending, at least it seems,
Like water torture,
Drip
Drip
Drip
Inane, insane,
Would someone please explain the
Mummy within,
The mummy without?
WOULD SOMEONE PLEASE EXPLAIN?

Suddenly I dream a dream so sane
That a glistening blade becomes
An object of beauty,
A rational thing - something to annihilate the
Drip
Drip
Drip
Rip, rip, rip…
Ahhhhhh finally
Sweet vermilion
Streaming down my skin;
Oh God, can letting go be quite so easy?
Or do I swoon, my stomach growing queasy?
My eyes light up,
I catch my breath…

Pregnant pause –

No, Death.
My life, at least, shall win out over you.

I drop the knife,
Heaving a groan,
And scramble hurriedly
For the telephone.

A Prayer for My Baby

Go gentle into that Good Light,
Feed on honey and flowers
From the meadows there,
And most of all, abandon care.
We now both know there was no fault,
Our times were simply out of joint.

Stay safely, snuggled
In my Nan's embracing lap;
Let the grace and love of Jesus
Guide you along your heavenly map;
And feel the love from my lips
Upon your precious head,
Each night as you lie upon
Your soft and downy bed.

Mostly, though, my angel heart,
Know that ours shall beat together
Through life and the Ever-after,
And fain will never part.

The Salad of the Bad Café

Each afternoon I'd roam the streets,
Searching for some dingy hole
To rest my soles, my aching feet;
The greasier the better,
The wetter the weather
To suit my mood:
My rude, angry, desperate
Mood.

Food, she'd said, you'll need
Instead of those countless
Butts that rot your gut.
Nuts, yoghurt, fruit and salad –
Do take care – see you next week.

So I'd try to listen
And be very good,
Just as I'd tried
My entire childhood.

But the rebellion was
Winning, fighting, grinning,
And as I lit a third cigarette,
I asked the waitress for a serviette
To go with my salad…my chips and peas,
And somewhere inside me
I felt rather pleased.

Headlines

Living alone in a bed,
For years at a time,
Can trigger deep yearnings
For a starving mind.

I switch on the radio to get the news,
To be part of the world, to hear
Correspondents' views: versions of news
Reported to a head easily confused.

    Taliban...
    Afghanistan...
    Pakistan...

Two mighty towers fall
And the world is changed forever.
These headlines reach my head
One innocent Tuesday morning;
These headlines hit my head
Without prior warning.

    Afghanistan...
    Taliban...
    Pakistan...

Anthrax, assassinations,
Bombing raids,
Civilian casualties,
Destruction, debris,
Enormous voids for nations;
...
Vainglorious terrorists planning
Zionist annihilation.

Pakistan...
Afghanistan...
Taliban...

All these lines wafting through my head -
These lines that instil outrage and dread;
These headlines that become increasingly blurred
As I switch constantly from Fourth to Third
Surfing the waves for some soothing refrain,
Some gentle harmony to soothe the pain
Of these headlines so frantic, repetitive, unclear;
Headlines that inspire only horror and fear.
Who knows what is truly taking place?
(It could well be news from outer space)
For all we really know below,
Below the Bombers, the B52s,
Beneath lies the truth, not the news.

Chocolate Porridge

Ahh... Mmmm... Mmm...
Mmm... O, god... Mmm... O...
Mm-Mm-O-Mm... there...
O-O... Mmmmmmmmmm –
Yes... Mmm... there is... O...
Mmmmm... a... Mmm... a...
O... Mmmmm... yes... Mmm...
Mmm... O... there is... Mmm...
A... Mmmmm... yes... yes
YES! – oh,

III Talking in Tongues

Mother Tongue

Two languages we seemed to speak:
What I thought to be English,
She, seemingly, ancient Greek.
Yet from her womb I sprang
And from her lips did learn
The incantations and rhythms
From an Anglo-Saxon urn.
At first we seemed to hear
The same melodies from this urn,
Nursery rhymes and stories,
The usual childhood churn.

Then one day something changed:
Somehow our language began to turn
In opposite directions -
Mine sought refuge in learning,
Hers in allowing truth to burn.
A knotted web she began to weave
Through my entire childhood,
A web of discordant, clashing threads,
A web I grew to hate and dread.
Yet she persisted in her spinning
Until the day a cocoon engulfed
Her betrayal and her sinning.

Inside this cocoon of deceit and lies
She was able to run and hide,
Not only from truth, but reality too,
And thus be deaf to my useless cries
To face the past, to hear again
The true language of her kin.

Stories and laughter we also shared:
My essays, thesis, poems I'd swear
I'd always written in my native tongue;
But in her cocoon, so finely spun,
Her language only would she hear.
Sadly, thus, we parted ways,
No longer of mutual understanding,
Plain English for her had now become
 far too demanding.

Now Marry in An Instant

Three parents had I while growing up,
The first two, Mom and Dad,
The third – well let's just simply call him Mad.

A right triumvirate they formed,
Though I recall only fallings out,
But nevertheless an unholy trinity that always shut me out.

A foreign language they seemed to speak
From shouts and cries, the occasional shriek;
To me it all seemed normal: familial Morse code.

My sister and I were always excluded
From their tight knit little group,
Yet all the time obeying orders from this fearsome troupe.

Until one day I flew away to the Land of Hope and Glory,
Hoping there to find a different language:
A way to express years of distress and dispel my early
    story.

Hoping, too, I have to say,
That the incestuous triumvirate – that trio of grown-up
    infants – would
Now marry in an instant.

Big Brother

Big brother was really very small,
Though looking up, he seemed twenty feet tall.

From the moment I was born
Big Brother hated my being.
To my parents, I their female delight,
To him, a usurper of his limelight.
So the seeds of jealousy grew,
Like those in that children's tale,
Until the Giant at the top became the keeper of my jail.

'Big Brother' he truly was – even in 1984,
The year before I finally learned how to say: NO MORE.

Up until then his beady eyes watched me like a hawk,
Fists beating me black and blue,
Ensuring I'd never talk.
Thus a television camera
Became the spy of my every move,
Its antennae the bug of my every word;
Asserting independence, therefore, was dangerous
    and absurd.

For Big Brother, of course, was always there –
Protruding from those malicious eyes a cautionary stare.

My true parents must have been around,
Though whenever I had the chance to look
Never could they be found.
So I too decided to vanish:
To find a place where those eyes were banished -
An imaginary realm to which I could escape,
And play with the butterflies while my body was
    raped.

Then one day Big Brother appeared like a big soapy bubble,
So I pricked him and he burst, no longer my source of
    trouble.

My parents, they never understood;
Even years later when the truth I told.
To them I had merely been transformed
Into a lying 'uncompassionate' being:
For refusing to relate any longer
To my tormenter, the 'Giant' abuser,
To his omnipresent SEEING.

Now Little Brother, though five years older than I,
It is your turn, at last, to be scrutinised directly in the eye.

Talking in Tongues

A seething little viper
Is how he considered her tongue,
Bathing in its venom,
And he the victim stung.

How it dared to wriggle
And dart directly at his face,
Still eludes this unhearing creature,
A blind man flinching from disgrace.

Miserably he'd carry himself,
A storm cloud ready to brew,
And all because his adult daughter
Lost at last her fear and dread,
And, like a volcano, began to spew.

The pile of vomit (Truth by any other name)
To him stinking, steaming poison
Which he could only label blame.
Never once did he consider he might bear the slightest
Responsibility for her body now chronically in pain.

Poor, poor man, so woebegone and cruelly abused,
"Excuse me, 'Sir', but I think you've got us both hopelessly confused",
To which he'd shrug his shoulders, pout his lips,
Sulk, his mouth all the while sucking the sourest of pips.

Ask for forgiveness, make amends?
These were tasks to which *he'd* never bend.
For she had committed the ultimate sin:
Dared to TELL of neglect, not respect,
And the hell her life had been.

So the daughter at last gave up:
She packed the bags of muffled moans
Of this self-pitying, surly grouch,
And sent him on his way,
Then used her tongue to better effect
That same and very day.

Alone

Alone, yet hasn't this always been the way?
Always the black sheep, the waif, the stray?
Then why now, twenty years on and ill three years,
Must this condition renew its cruelty,
Springing forth torrents of tears?

A mirror imaging my younger days,
Reflecting its injustice, resonating with pain,
This disease pinning me to my bed –
A similar jailkeeper, a being insane;
Alone I lie ravaged again and again…

Perhaps that is in part the reason why:
Our reflections only age, never die.
Yet my imprisonment this time *is* different –
My jailkeeper has fled never to return -
Thus in this state, alone, I've a chance to learn.

I am now safe in this different bed,
Safe and free from that fearsome dread,
With time to heal, to change, to become me,
To create new beginnings
And, ironically, to be free.

The Mute Bard

He sat on the bed, his back to her,
Words gliding over his ears;
When she would plead
He'd a quarter turn,
Afraid to face her tears.
But she, determined, soldiered on,
Unpacking the pain of years.

He, the mute bard, author of
Numerous books, had suddenly
Lost his tongue, and with it
Compassion and fatherly love
For his very own: his young.
So, the man of millions of words,
The world-renowned scholar,
Could not for a single minute
Find one syllable to address his daughter.

Still she persisted, having lost all fear,
(That awe instilled when we are small,)
And told him of her time as a child,
Her neglect, her abuse,
Even as she crawled.
Now great earplugs stopped his ears,
Like those he wore when she grew up,
Until finally she knew
They were permanently stuck.
And in the end she had to laugh,
Realising her father a photograph.

In My Day

'I would never have spoken
To my parents in that way;
In my day we knew respect,
How to deflect the things they had
No right to say.'

Today I never speak to my parents
In any way at all, for none
Is acceptable except the creep and crawl,
To which I shall never stoop, even when I am old.
No matter what age, my own children shall never be
Frightened to scold, cry, fly off the handle,
Or to have their stories told.

C# Major

Somewhere deep inside that man
Is still the kernel from which I grew.

Somewhere deep inside that head
Lies the father I once knew.

Somewhere dormant within his heart
Is locked a love so deep it hurts.

Somewhere within that brooding brow
Hangs the key: C# major that may unlock me.

Under My Battlements

'The raven himself is hoarse',
Cries Lady Macbeth, 'That croaks
the fatal entrance...' of
Truth under my mother's
'Battlements'; for in a
Structure like Inverness
Dwells she, screwing up her
Children, not her courage,
And stopping up any
'Visitings of nature' to inhabit
Her Queendom of hell.

So the murder of innocence was
   allowed to dwell,
And the rape of her babes
Was, like a dagger, nothing
'Unnatural'. Slaughtering
Future lives – perfectly normal,
The Lady once said,
Especially for girls –
Think nothing of it – for that
Only leads to Truth which
Peeping through heaven,
Reveals dirty deeds.

Under my mother's battlements
I was forced to live,
And never once reveal
The secrets she knew best.
An obsession, though, soon emerged,
With her 'dirty hands':
Scrub, scrape, clean, shake,
Nothing would remove the taint
That concealed her psychopathic saint.
All the perfumes of Arabia,
And even the Clarins counter,
Unsurprisingly had no effect,
The problem being of course,
A deep mental defect.

I, myself, when older,
With clean and guiding hands,
Told her that pacing in her gown
Would only wear her down.
In earnest did I pray
For my mother to get help;
Alas, she laughed and washed her hands,
Uttering a yelp – a yelp
That echoed through and through
Battlements that only grew.

The Cat's Cow

After seven years of deep, deep, sleep,
The black cat awoke and began to creep
Around her house she knew so well,
Into every corner did she delve.
Sniffing old haunts she looked everywhere
For her silver bowl and tin
Filled, she hoped, with her favourite food:
Turkey and speckled hen.
But her owner was nowhere to be found -
Simply vanished - most likely flying around.
So the cat waited and waited
Until she could no more,
When suddenly she spied,
Standing next to the door,
Her owner's old broomstick -
Covered in cobwebs now -
And on top of it stood
A jar of pickled cow.
Pickled cow? The cat meowed,
YUK! I don't want that.
The least she could have done
Was leave me a meal homespun.
But she was a witch after all,
And nine lives *she* had not,
However powerful her spells she thought.
So the cat left in grand indignation
To seek a new life
And tastier salvation.

The Languages of Silence

Silence can speak louder than words,
So the aphorism said;
Silence, for me, only amplified words
In my mute upside down head.
Wordless pleas, sobs and moans:
The language of pain so often locked in,
For many like me, imprisoned sin.

At school I studied Latin,
A splash of ancient Greek,
Ironically these 'dead' languages were much safer to
  speak.
Fluent in French by the age of seven,
Honours and ribbons at graduation.
English, a toy, with which I was allowed to play,
I now doubt how eagerly they'd have let me
Had they known just how much
One day I'd have to say.

But for a while languages served me well,
Excelling through three degrees;
Accolades and scholarships kept me fooled -
How easily was I then pleased.
Until such a time it came to pass
That no further in academe could I last:
My mouth had gone dry, my future awry,
And it started to dawn on me
The true reason why.

Words, words, words –
They were the reason why;
And, like Hamlet, I could see
There was more to life than philosophy.
I had never had my say
To the people who needed it most,
I had never appeased the raging silence:
The thirty-year family ghost.

So I tried and cried,
Screamed and shouted,
Then talked and TOLD – the act most bold –
But I was soon to find
Their ears cut off from their heads,
Rather like that painter sublime,
Only their ears vanished to erase a crime.
Thus, my language, once so heavily lauded,
Had become to them a tongue most fraudulent.

None of that bothers me now -
For my words still can be read,
In silence, hopefully, right before bed.

Cappuccino Talk

Sitting over cappuccinos,
Trading tastes of sinful delights,
I'd look into your face
Searching for some ray of light.
Suddenly I'd want to stroke your hand
And say that all was well,
But sitting, sipping coffee,
Our distance only deepened,
Drawn from a similar well.

The aching grew in my heart,
My furtive desire to tell
That I knew exactly how you felt;
But your glazed eyes
Warned me always:
In that place do not dwell.
So I'd eat the sugar first
You the foamy bit last,
And from such simple gestures
A slight but subtle contrast:
I desiring an immediate resolution,
You too entrenched by sixty years
To ever ponder a solution.

Mother and daughter,
Coffee and chatter,
Nonsense, froth and laughter;
But, sadly, emptiness after.
Thus a possible truth between us -
An intimate bond to share –
Is layer by layer smoothed over
Like sedimentary rock,
Like cappuccino talk.

Animal Noises

Twit, twit, twoo,
Said the owl to the hen,
Quickly, twitted the owl,
While the grown-ups are away.
So the hen heavily lumbered
Unwillingly to his nest,
Twit, twit, twoo,
No need to explain the rest.

Oink, oink, kick, wink,
O God, here he goes again,
Everyday a secret reminder
Of the same painful ritual;
Oink, oink, kick, wink,

OINK, OINK, KICK, KICK,
So I'd lumber to his room,
And lie, a dead body, in his tomb.

Only the codes ever changed,
From animal grunts to a well-hidden punch,
From pulling faces to whispered threats,
The language of his body,
Sadly, the only promise ever kept.
And I had never any choice
But to collude with this tyrant they called my
  brother,
As I searched frantically every time for sight
  of my mother.

The Tower of Babel

Philomela had hers cut off
In case she ever told;
I had mine anaesthetised
As he knew I could be bold.

But the clever woman,
Perhaps by the light of the moon,
Was undeterred and wove her story
To her sister with a simple loom.

At an early age I too
Discovered the power of the written word,
But alas my treachery he'd often spy
And rip my missives or have them burned.

For such acts of babbling
To the Tower I'd be forced,
Bound, gagged and left in the dark,
Threatened if I told, my parents would divorce.

So I also learned the power of silence,
And sought my refuge in libraries
Where real books –printed and bound –
Offered hushed safety and 'proper' stories.

What I learned there was a true blessing:
One day by the might of the pen,
I, like Philomela, could use my power
And write my story again,
This time free as a Nightingale,
Winging my way from the Tower
To my own literary heaven.

The Circle Game

Round and round and round we go,
Playing this game of being in the know –
The know-go, no-don't-go,
Oh please don't go there, at least for now.

Now soon turns into next week,
Next week, next month, my god it's a year;
Oh please, please yet another year – so
I can keep up my run – swim – ride and hide.

Round and round the track I go –
So fast now, nobody will know
What you know and are trying so hard
To make me reveal – it's just… it's just
You see, I can no longer feel.
So I shall run and run my life away,
Perhaps 'til I'm eighty – it's possible they say;
I shall make my career trying to veer
From what you so urgently wish me to face –
The disgrace from our past, the one we both share –
Just please, goddam it, stop trying to care.

So round and round and round we go,
You too ill, I too dizzy, too busy to be fair;
So let's turn this circle into a square:
Edgy, hedgy, able to hide – at least for now so I may decide.

Sorry?

Sorry is no longer a word;
Perhaps it is a bird
That flies so high in the sky
It's imperceptible to the eye.

Sorry is not in our language,
Despite its power to bandage
Our gaping, aching wounds,
To heal and revive our swoons.

Its disappearance is a mystery
In a family of so much history –
English history and lore –
'Sorry' appears no more.

Perhaps it was the delete key,
That so quickly erases memory.
The technology of this age
Has buried sorry deep in a grave.

I'm so confused that sorry is dead,
For it continues to live in *my* head –
Thriving, in fact, within my ken -
Willing to slip off my tongue or pen.

Sorry, then, my dearest kin,
I'm beginning to think
Your vocabulary is wearing thin,
As I heard 'sorry' only the other day,
On the radio it was, in a play.
The play amazingly,
You'll never guess…
Was called *The Sorry Story*,
A children's play –
Perhaps you'll understand it best that way.

Inspector Morse Isn't Dead

All day long I've been battling a song,
A song in my head filled with codeine
    and dread,
Filled with shock and horror,
Horror at the song in my head
That goes: 'Inspector Morse isn't dead,
Isn't dead, Isn't dead –
He's at my home looking under the bed,
Under the bed, Under the bed,
To check if anyone is dead.'

'Inspector Morse isn't dead –
Isn't dead, Isn't dead…'
How could he be when he's
Gathering evidence against a paedophile –
A paedophile in a family, oh so well read,
So well read that they'll be
Damned if any body could be found
Under one of their beds - found
Under one of their well–red beds.

Yet this song still persists, despite
The obvious, despite the evidence
Of all the bodies being found
Under family or camp-beds;
Inspector Morse is NOT DEAD,
Goddam it, though they showed it on T.V.:
Everyone seemed to see it…
That is, except me. I guess
I was too busy trying to
Chase away the song – the song
That isn't wrong – the song
Whose hero may not be a famous one,
But nevertheless a good and honest man,
Trying to stop injustice, trying
To stop a paedophile from further harm
    and scam.
So finally I unstop my ears and shake the
    detective's hand.

Forgive Me

Angel girl, so tall, so slim,
I'm just so sorry you've become
A character from the Brothers Grimm;
A character perhaps is too understated –
What I mean is a victim too underrated.

Over my head, my heart, my soul,
Lies guilt: the silence of my mouth.
For that, angel, the most heinous toll
Paid by you, so young; so unjust
That I've lost my faith, my trust.

Forgive my cowardice, my fear, my running;
I was then only trying my best to survive
The same toll that you had to pay,
The same scarring etched in my spirit today.
That I ran so far, though, is the reason I'm still alive.

If 'should' could only wipe a slate clean,
If 'should' could eradicate scenes so obscene.
All I can say is that with all my heart
I'm sorry I never warned fully and was so scared.
But please believe my love for you is always there,
Despite the indelible ink that now has etched the crime.

Let us pray that hopefully you may give voice to it in time,
And so unburden your pain, your anger, in your words, unashamed,
Forever after living in the realm of Angels' radiant shine.

The Key to the Sea

Had I known the depths of your evil
mind – the grime and slime of that
ruined mine of duplicity, threats,
abuse and crime; had I known the
profundity of your scheming,
underhanded, meticulous crimes,
beyond the age when I had done my
own time, I would have handed your
head on a silver platter to the proper
authorities – the ones who matter –
who deal everyday with such filth
splattered – I would have smeared
your grey matter across the papers;
I would have had you locked up and
thrown away the key to the wolves, to
the vultures of discarded decaying
carcasses. But illness, caused, by
the way, by you, for years until now
has prevented that glee – that glee of
throwing away the key: the rusty,
ugly, massive key – I envision from
my bed being flung into the sea.
O fathomless sea – bury that key
3000 under, then wash me clean –
my childhood scenes so obscene, my
tarnished spirit, my bleeding heart.
Mighty ocean of this entire planet:
wash others clean too: those whose
crimes they also cannot undo. Wash
us all in your purifying lotion – purge
us with your salty devotion - O I pray,
great mystical ocean.

The Go Away Game
For Peta

A wise kind woman once said to me,
If you wish to be done with the past,
There are many methods to be free;
One, of course, is to forgive, then forget;
(That method I wasn't ready for yet.)
Another one is the 'Go Away' game:
It has worked wonders for many
And it does not involve blame.

Just as thought creeps in through a door,
Many will trail, following those more;
For each thought we have
Pulls open a gate to let in another,
Then another and another as before.
Shut that gate, at the very first hint,
And firmly say: GO AWAY, GO AWAY -
If you must, come back another day.

The idea first struck me as rather childish:
Pushing down thoughts into our subconscious
Surely would make them grow more wildish,
Trying at any opportune moment
To leap out and strike you down in one blow.
But the wisdom of the woman
I respected greatly, so I gave it a try
And to my surprise, gates remained closed
Before my inner eyes.

It dawned on me then that I must
Throw away my former thinking –
A task not simple, like stopping one's blinking.
But if the *first* thought is constantly reminded,
The rest behind will similarly be chided.
So through time and visual graphics
I changed the route of my painful traffic.
Now if ever unwanted thoughts will climb
Over forbidden gates - like a crime -
I simply say: GO AWAY, GO AWAY,
And the thoughts will then amazingly transform,
Finding their resting place in some alternate form.

Losing Brine

Water
dripping from a fountain
drops not needing a mop
to soak up my salty tears
streaming faster down my cheeks
for years of tears never spilt
for years of words never said
stories and poems you never read
the bread of life, only *my* life
thus words invisible, my heart risible
blood flowing through veins
forget the brain which now reigns
rains... splatter, splatter,
splashes my grey matter
dripping streaming glistening
reflecting the matter at hand:
my water land –
drops of slaughter
slaughter of a daughter
drops now dissolving crime
drops now losing brine
like water growing
softer.

Other books in the 'Poet of the Season' series include:

'Stanza Chance' by Bob Griffiths   *ISBN 1-902628-10-1*
The first *'Poet of the Season'* in this programme is an ex-helicopter pilot from Devon whose collection shows a remarkable insight into life, love and thoughts. (The poet was subsequently invited to read his poems on Devon Radio).

'The Hour-Glass' by Sarah Collett   *ISBN 1-902628-11-X*
Sarah Collett wrote this amazing collection as a schoolgirl on the borders of Wiltshire and Gloucestershire. For one so young, she writes with intense feeling and emotion. Beneath her pen she creates words of immense power to describe the merest whispers.

'Hope to Defeat' by Rhona Johnston   *ISBN 1-902628-12-8*
Rhona Johnston was a long-distance runner who was suddenly struck down by the dreaded anorexia nervosa. In this collection of moving poems she writes despairingly and hauntingly of her spirited recovery.

'A Pillow Book' by Yvonne Eve Walus   *ISBN 1-902628-13-6*
A worthy collection of poems by the talented South African writer who remarkably, without bias or favour, has previously been published as *'Author of Our Times'* and *'Writer of the Future'*.

'Les Deux Poetes Français' translated by Reine Errington   *ISBN 1-902628-14-4*
This *'Poet of the Season'* is not one, but two poets, neither English, but both French and long since dead. But the work of the sixteenth century poets, Joachim du Bellay and Pierre Ronsard, now sensitively translated by Reine Errington, takes us into a very different country in a very different age. Yet there is something strangely familiar within their rural settings. It is like discovering an early Shakespearean manuscript.

'Blinkers Off' by Jean Frances   *ISBN 1-902628-15-2*
Jean Frances was born in England and emigrated to Australia. She saw the world with new eyes. This is her heartfelt story.

'Catch Me If You Can' by Sue Fincham   *ISBN 1-902628-16-0*
The revealing loves, the hopes, the hates, the fears, the thoughts and the yearnings of a lady who lives by the sea in beautiful Norfolk

'Signals in the Dark' by Sylvia Downes   *ISBN 1-902628-17-9*
Revelations to stimulate the intellect as well as the emotions from a well-travelled, observant lady.

'Augmented Seventh' by Gwyneth Hughes   *ISBN 1-902628-18-7*
Gwyneth Hughes works in the theatre in Paris, and colourfully describes her experiences through this collection of poetry.

'Desert Anthems' Translated by Talaal M. Omer   *ISBN 1-902628-19-5*
Poetry is the Council of the Arabs, and so Talaal Omer translated these works of the Immortal Arab Poets to transport the reader into their hot, colourful, enchanting worlds.

'Travels in the Antipodes' by Jacqueline Crompton Ottaway   *ISBN 1-902628-38-1*
A collection of poems which takes the reader on a beautiful journey through Heaven on Earth . . .

'What Women Talk About' by Tonie Watts   *ISBN 1-902628-29-2*
Not only what women talk about, but what women think and what women feel, written by a woman whose intellect should not be underestimated.

'Bees in My Bonnet' by Isabella Strachan   *ISBN 1-902628-37-3*
Isabella Strachan has an uncanny aptitude for seeing everyday events in their historical perspective which adds a certain realism to this collection of poems.

'Recitable Rhymes' by Alan Millard   *ISBN 1-902628-39-X*
This is a brilliant collection of humorous poems by a witty writer which can be recited for any of many occasions.

The above works are available in one comprehensive volume
entitled 'All Our Poets of the Season', available to readers of this
chapbook directly from the publisher at special discount price.